The Tremendous Tudors Quiz Book

England's King and Queens - 1485-1603.

By

Joanne Hayle

Questions

Henry Tudor, the first Tudor king, was born at Pembroke Castle in Wales on 28th January 1457. What was he known as in Welsh?

Harri Tudur.

Tuddy ap Gyndwr.

Harrold a Castell Penfro.

What title did the future King Henry VII hold before he battled his way to the throne?

Earl of Rutland.

Earl of Richmond.

Earl of Reading.

Who was Henry's father, a half brother of King Henry VI?

Edmund Tudor.

Edward Tudor.

Edwin Tudor.

How old was Henry's mother Margaret Beaufort when she became a widow, whilst still pregnant with Henry?

13 years old.

15 years old.

17 years old.

Henry's late paternal grandmother Catherine de Valois was queen consort to which monarch during her first marriage?

King Henry III.

King Henry IV.

King Henry V.

Henry became the senior male heir in which house?

Lancaster.

York.

Stuart.

His uncle Jasper Tudor rushed an adolescent Henry to which area of France for his safety? He remained there for thirteen years.

Brittany.

Normandy.

Aquitaine.

When Henry travelled to his homeland to claim the throne in 1485, where did his ship moor?

Milford Haven, Wales.

Whitby, north east England.

Plymouth, south west England.

Which battle was fought on the 22nd August 1485? It resulted in King Richard III's death and Henry being proclaimed the new king whilst still on the battlefield.

Battle of Towton.

Battle of Berwick Moor.

Battle of Bosworth Field.

Who placed the crown on Henry's head that day?

His uncle Jasper Tudor.

His stepfather Lord Thomas Stanley.

His mother Margaret Beaufort.

Who did Henry marry on 18th January 1486 at
Westminster Abbey?

Elizabeth of York.

Elizabeth of Lancaster.

Elizabeth of Scotland.

Which emblem was created to mark this union, an
end to the decades of dispute about who should rule
the country, the Wars of the Roses?

The White Hart.

The Tudor Rose.

The Lion of England.

Name the two best known claimants to the throne who vowed that they were the late King Edward IV's nephew Edward, and Edward IV's second son Richard. Neither succeeded in overthrowing Henry VII.

Lambert Simnel and Perkin Warbeck.

Lionel Brookes and Patrick Clements.

Ludovic Swaine and John Mcgee.

Henry used high taxation, fines and land confiscation

from his more wealthy subjects as devices to ensure that no one had the resources to challenge his power.

True.

False.

When Henry VIII became king in 1509 what did he do to his father's chief tax collectors Edmund Dudley and Richard Empson?

Employed them to instigate more severe taxation measures.

He executed them for treason on trumped up charges.

Pensioned them off, giving them land in Ireland.

Henry VII lost his wife on the 11th February of which year? This was the day after the death of their nine day old daughter Katherine.

1407.

1405.

1403.

Where is the chapel built in his name and completed in 1516, that has provided a magnificent resting place for several royals including himself and his wife, his grandchildren Edward VI, Mary I and Elizabeth I?

St. Paul's Cathedral.

Westminster Abbey.

Welbeck Abbey.

Henry was how old when he passed away on 21st April 1509 at Richmond Palace?

42 years old.

52 years old.

72 years old.

When did Henry's mother Margaret Beaufort die?

27th September 1516.

28th April 1512.

29th June 1509.

Who did Sir Roland de Velville, Constable of
Beaumaris Castle between 1509 and 1535, claim to
be?

Henry VII's illegitimate son, born in 1474 to a
Frenchwoman.

Richard III's illegitimate son and a claimant to the
throne, born in 1484.

Edward Plantagenet, Earl of Warwick, Richard III's
nephew, born in 1475. He had been living in England
under another identity.

Is this portrait of Henry VII, his eldest son Arthur or his second son Henry?

In 1485 Henry created the military corps of Ordinary

and extraordinary guards stationed at the Tower of London. They are still popularly known as Beefeaters and wear a distinct uniform. What was and is their shortened title?

The Yeoman of the Guard.

The Wardens of the Tower.

The Yeoman Warders.

The future King Henry VIII was born at Greenwich Palace in London on which date?

27th January 1489.

28th June 1491.

29th July 1493.

Who was the youngest son of Henry VII and Elizabeth of York?

Henry.

Arthur.

Edmund.

Henry VIII's maternal grandmother was which queen?

Margaret of Anjou.

Elizabeth Woodville.

Anne Neville.

His maternal grandfather was which king of England?

Edward IV.

Edward III.

Edward II.

Aged three, which title was Henry awarded?

Duke of Kent.

Prince of Wales.

Duke of York.

Which scholar, philosopher and friend of Sir Thomas
More met a nine year old Prince Henry and thought
that he had a "certain dignity and singular courtesy"
but in later life became wary and disapproving of
him?

Desiderious Erasmus.

Voltaire (Francois-Marie Arouet.)

Rene Descartes.

Henry was a highly intelligent boy, a keen student
and an avid reader.

True.

False.

Which of these activities was Henry *not* good at?

Dancing.

Music.

Conjuring.

How many years after Prince Arthur's death on 2nd April 1502 was Henry created the Prince of Wales and Earl of Chester by his father?

Within one year, on 18th February 1503.

Two years later, on 2nd April 1504.

Five years later, on 28th June 1508.

Which sport did Henry excel at although his father wished that he would not participate because it was dangerous?

Jousting.

Bare knuckle fighting.

Fencing.

How many horses did a contemporary state that the young Henry could tire out during one day's hunting?

Two.

Five.

Ten.

On which date did Henry VIII succeed to the throne?

21st April 1507.

21st April 1509.

21st April 1510.

Which piece of music is Henry VIII credited with composing even though he didn't?

Greensleeves.

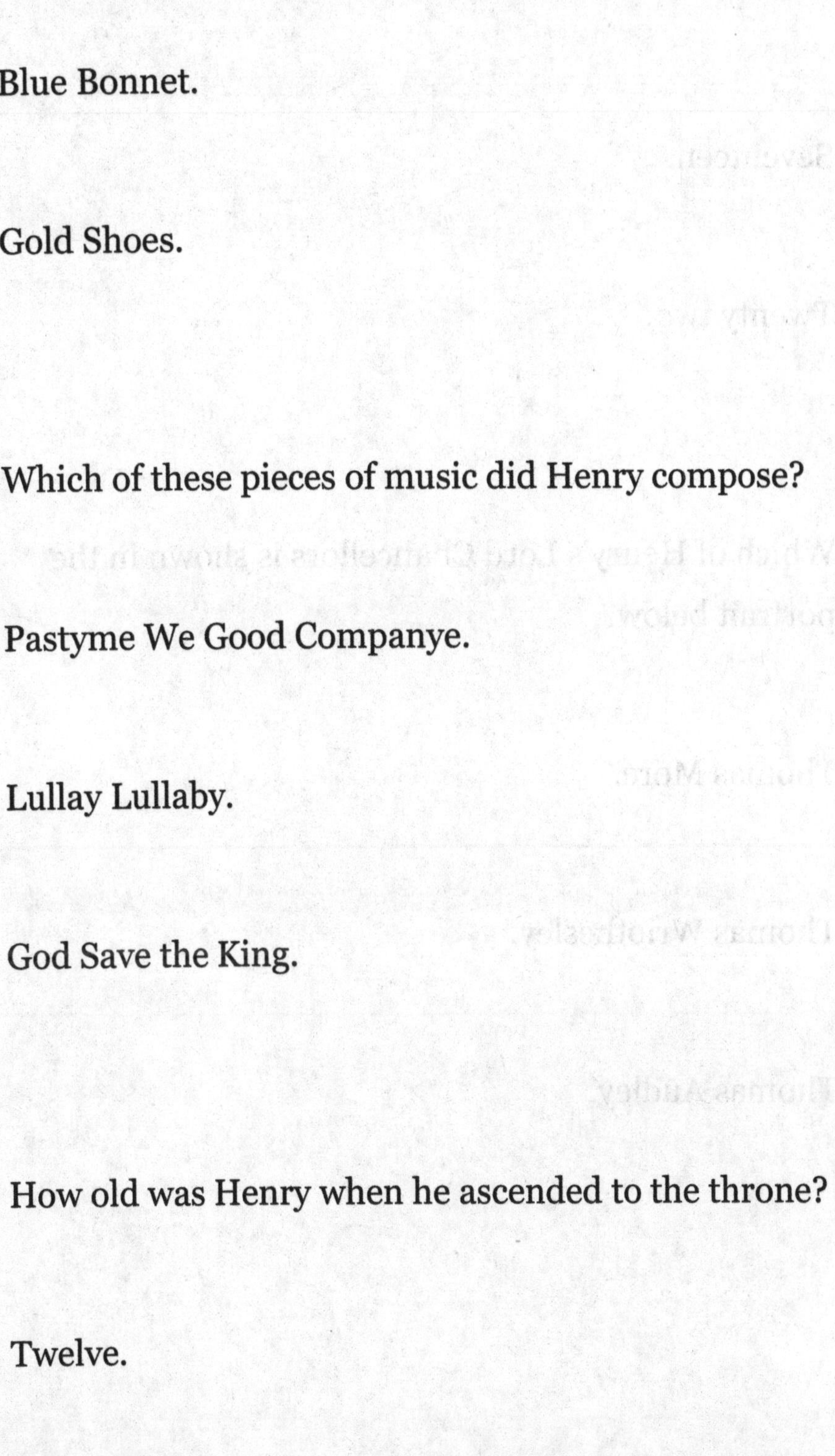

Blue Bonnet.

Gold Shoes.

Which of these pieces of music did Henry compose?

Pastyme We Good Companye.

Lullay Lullaby.

God Save the King.

How old was Henry when he ascended to the throne?

Twelve.

Seventeen.

Twenty two.

Which of Henry's Lord Chancellors is shown in the portrait below?

Thomas More.

Thomas Wriothesley.

Thomas Audley.

How many wives did Henry VIII have?

Six.

Seven.

Eight.

How many of Henry's wives were beheaded?

One.

Two.

Three.

Who did Henry marry on 11th June 1509?

Catherine of Aragon.

Katherine Parr.

Katherine Howard.

What relation was the bride to him?

Sister in law.

First cousin.

Fourth cousin, once removed.

On which day did the couple have their coronation at Westminster Abbey?

11th June 1509.

23rd June 1509.

28th June 1509.

What name was given to their tragically short lived son, born on New Year's Day 1511? (And to two other issue who passed away within hours or were stillborn.)

Arthur.

Edward.

Henry.

What was the name of Henry VIII's eldest legitimate daughter born on 18th February 1516?

Elizabeth.

Mary.

Catherine.

Courtier Bessie (Elizabeth) Blount was Henry's long term unofficial mistress. She was the mother of his illegitimate son Henry Fitzroy, born on 15th June 1519. What title was bestowed on the boy in 1525?

Earl of Abingdon and Oxford.

Viscount Reading and Windsor.

Duke of Richmond and Somerset.

What happened to this son Henry?

He died as a teenager and was genuinely mourned by Henry VIII.

He was made legitimate by Henry VIII and became king after him.

He tried to seize the throne when he was twenty five and was executed for treason.

A celebration-tournament of peace and friendship with frequent foe France was held in Balinghem in Northern France during June 1520. What was the event called?

The Tournament of Peace and Goodwill.

The Triumph of the Golden Fleece.

The Field of the Cloth of Gold.

Shown in this portrait, who was king of France during this event?

Louis XII.

François I.

Charles X.

Who gave Henry VIII the title Defender of the Faith?

Pope Leo X.

William Warham, the Archbishop of Canterbury.

Henry awarded it to himself.

Which London palace was built on the orders of
Henry VIII in the 1530's?

Buckingham Palace.

St. James' Palace.

Greenwich Palace.

What had sat on the land prior to the palace?

A brewery.

A hospital.

A cattle market.

Which college did Henry create at Cambridge
University?

Trinity College.

King's College.

Corpus Christi College.

As an adult Henry's height was commented on as unusual. Was he...?

Below five feet tall.

Approximately five feet five inches tall.

Over six feet tall.

Which of Henry's numerous palaces is shown in the image below?

Greenwich Palace.

Hampton Court Palace.

Eltham Palace.

What other name was this palace known by?

Palace of Placentia.

Palace ad Infinitum.

Palace Se Defendendo.

Why did Henry's first marriage end in acrimony?

After first accepting that her husband would be
unfaithful, the queen hated that his mistresses had
more power than her. He grew tired of her anger. She
grew weary of being ignored.

Henry was desperate to make a new dynastic match
to prevent a costly war in Europe. Divorce was
deemed less expensive and less dramatic.

After over twenty years of marriage there was no
surviving male heir to succeed Henry. He decided

that Catherine had to be replaced because their marriage was not blessed and so he would not have a living son with her.

Henry's Lord Chancellor was given the unenviable task of achieving a divorce through the Pope so that the king could remarry. Who was he?

Thomas Cromwell.

Thomas Wolsey.

Thomas Seymour.

What was the name given at court to the question of Henry's divorce and remarriage?

The King's Great Matter.

The King's Conundrum.

The King's Malady.

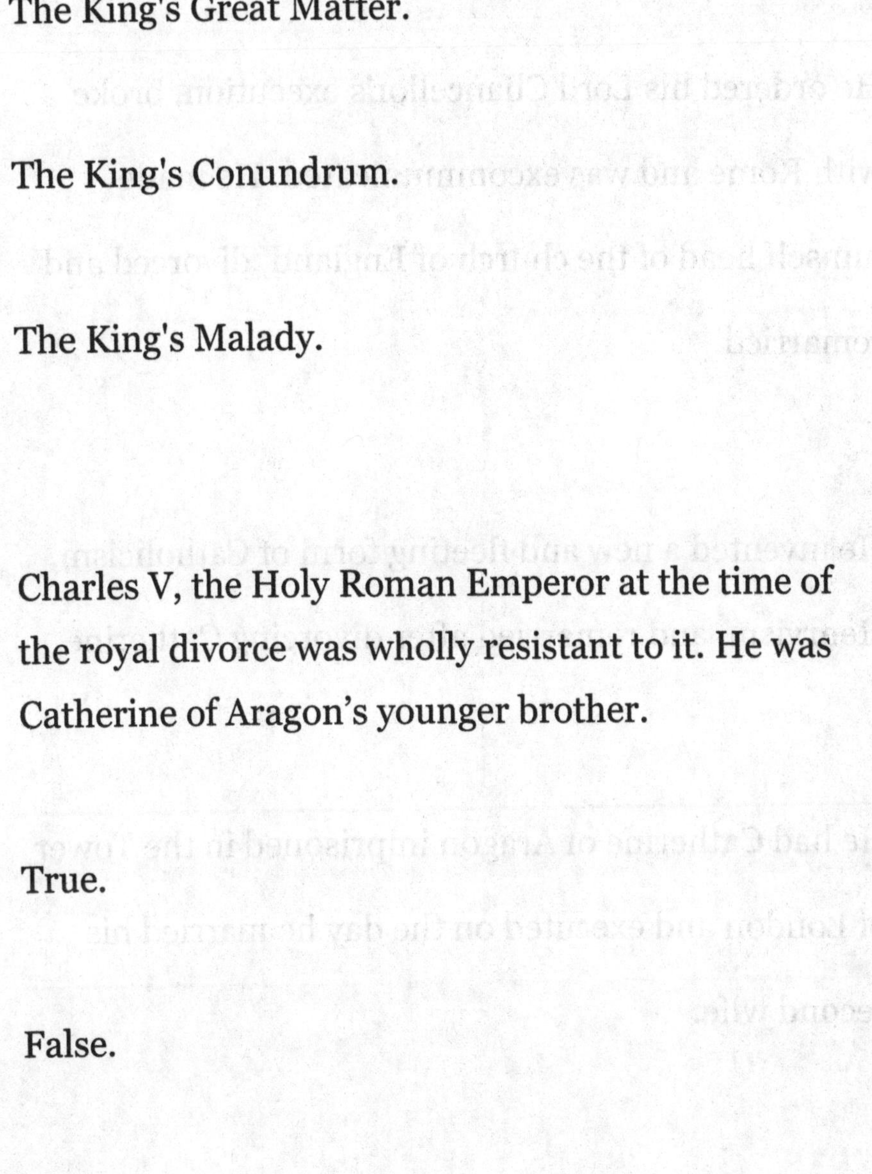

Charles V, the Holy Roman Emperor at the time of
the royal divorce was wholly resistant to it. He was
Catherine of Aragon's younger brother.

True.

False.

When a divorce could not be secured through the
Pope what did Henry VIII do?

He ordered his Lord Chancellor's execution, broke with Rome and was excommunicated. He made himself head of the church of England, divorced and remarried.

He invented a new and fleeting form of Catholicism, Henryism, and remarried after divorcing Catherine.

He had Catherine of Aragon imprisoned in the Tower of London and executed on the day he married his second wife.

What name was given to this period in Tudor history?

The English Restoration.

The English Reformation.

The English Refinement.

The Dissolution of the Monasteries, the destruction and sale of church land and property throughout the late 1530's and early 1540's was vital in Henry's eyes to his success. Why?

The Catholic church owned vast amounts of land in England and the monks were loyal to the Pope. They posed a significant threat to Henry's power. Henry wanted the land in the ownership of his loyal courtiers.

He needed to raise funds for war with France. The Dissolution paid for home defences and soldiers wages.

Henry wanted to use the money raised from the Dissolution to negotiate and pay handsomely for the dynastic marriage of his daughter Mary to Philip of Spain.

Henry's second wife was Anne Boleyn. What was the name of the daughter they had together?

Eleanor.

Margaret.

Elizabeth.

What did the Pilgrimage of Grace, an uprising in 1536, call for?

The King to abdicate so that papal power could be restored under a worthy monarch.

Thomas Cromwell's dismissal as Henry's chief minister. He was the architect of the tumultuous changes in policies and religion.

Anne Boleyn's banishment. Her presence in Henry's life was considered the cause and the solution to the unrest.

Why did Henry end his marriage to Anne?

She miscarried a son and Henry was persuaded to believe that she had bewitched him in to marriage and that she would not bear a son.

Henry was told that she wished to assassinate him and rule with the House of Norfolk.

Henry learned that she had schemed with Charles V and the Pope to regain favour in case she was discarded or the king overthrown.

What other charge was levelled against her?

Incest with her uncle Thomas Howard, 3rd Duke of Norfolk.

Incest with her brother George Boleyn, Viscount Rochford.

That she had cheated on Henry with Charles V, the Holy Roman Emperor.

Anne Boleyn faced trial in May 1536. Who, as Earl Marshal of England was one of the most powerful men present; he delivered the sentence of execution to Anne with no apparent qualms?

Her uncle Thomas Howard, 3rd Duke of Norfolk.

Her brother George Boleyn, Viscount Rochford.

Her father Thomas Boleyn, Earl of Wiltshire.

At the tower of London, how was Anne executed?

Her head was severed from her body with a sword not an axe, said to be an act of kindness from Henry VIII.

Henry arranged that she was hung, drawn and quartered without a crowd present.

Anne was stretched on the rack until broken and her body held aloft to show her demise. The king turned away at the sight.

What date was Anne Boleyn executed on?

19th May 1536.

29th July 1537.

9th September 1538.

Thomas Wolsey was replaced as Lord Chancellor by which man who would later be executed by Henry?

Sir Thomas More.

Sir William Cavendish.

Sir William Wriothesley.

What date did Henry's first wife Catherine of Aragon die on?

1st January 1534.

5th January 1535.

7th January 1536.

Which of these forces was Henry VIII credited with expanding substantially during his reign?

The Army.

The Navy.

The Home Guard.

What was the name of the famous Tudor ship that first sailed in 1511, was refurbished in 1536 and sank in battle in 1545?

Mary Tudor.

Mary Stuart.

Mary Rose.

What was the sister ship of the above called?

Peter Pomegranate.

Patricia Potato.

Paul Papaya.

Cook Richard Roose was found guilty of poisoning his employer, John Fisher, the Bishop of Rochester in 1531 and also of killing two other diners. The bishop survived. What punishment did Henry decide was appropriate for the cook?

He was made to ingest poison and died a slow, painful death.

He was publicly boiled alive.

He was set to work as a lowly servant in Henry's households, given the worst tasks and never permitted to cook again.

This is a portrait of Elizabeth, daughter of Anne Boleyn and Henry VIII.

True.

False.

What happened to Henry VIII on 24th January 1536</sup>

during a jousting tournament that he was participating in at Greenwich Palace?

Whilst competing, Henry fell and his horse landed on him. After a few hours of unconsciousness the king, who was thought to be dying, awoke. He was left with a painful ulcer on his leg which never recovered and his manner from this point became more aggressive.

Henry was allowed to win by his courtiers and jousters. He found out that he had not won honourably and was livid. He swore never to joust again if he could not have fair competitions.

Henry survived an assassination attempt in which the tip of his opponent's lance had a small dagger attached. The plot failed and the would-be assassin was hung, drawn and quartered.

Who was Henry VIII's third wife?

Anne of Cleves.

Katherine Parr.

Jane Seymour.

This queen bore him a son on 12th October 1537 but died from complications within days. What was the son's name?

Henry.

Edward.

Edmund.

Who was appointed Archbishop of Canterbury in 1533 and held the role for twenty two years until tried for heresy and burned at the stake?

Thomas Cromwell.

Thomas Cranmer.

Thomas Wriothesley.

Is this portrait of...?

Cromwell.

Cranmer.

Wriothesley.

Henry VIII placed his infant son in the care of Mary and Elizabeth's Lady Governess. What was her name?

Lady Frances Rochford.

Lady Ursula Stafford.

Lady Margaret Bryan.

What did Henry's 1535 and 1542 Laws in Wales Acts do?

Officially united Wales and England in to a single territory.

Gave Wales its own parliament which did not answer to London's Westminster parliament, just to the monarch.

Each act allowed the Welsh landowners to keep all farming revenue, untaxed for a three year period of grace. (Then Henry raised taxes so the benefit was minimal.)

How did Henry VIII acquire the nickname Coppernose?

Some of the coins that Henry commissioned and placed in circulation had a flaw. When the silver gilt on the king's nose was rubbed it wore off to show that copper, a less expensive metal, lay beneath.

He had a habit of wearing copper toned makeup that made him look healthy and invincible so that his friends and enemies would believe that he was not ageing.

A copper statue was crafted and presented to the king by an artist craving patronage. Unfortunately, it depicted Henry with a large hook nose. The artist was imprisoned rather than patronised.

What nickname was given to Henry's fourth wife
Anne of Cleves?

The Flemish Hare.

The French Shrew.

The Flanders Mare.

Who painted the portrait of Anne of Cleves that
Thomas Cromwell presented to Henry VIII when
persuading him to marry once again?

Hans Holbein.

Antony Van Dyke.

Sir Joshua Reynolds.

In Summer 1540 how did Henry VIII thank Cromwell for arranging the marriage?

He was stripped of his authority and banished to his country estates.

He was rewarded with a dukedom.

He was executed and his head displayed on a spike at London Bridge.

After an unsuccessful few months of marriage Henry demanded an annulment, which Anne of Cleves wisely agreed to. They remained friendly for the remainder of their lives and Henry called Anne which of the following?

The King's Merciful Wife.

The King's Beloved Sister.

The King's Mother of Virtue.

With the annulment, Anne was awarded properties including which castle, once home to Henry's second wife's family?

Hever Castle.

Arundel Castle.

Pembroke Castle.

Who was Henry's fifth wife? She was a niece of the 3rd Duke of Norfolk and a cousin of Anne Boleyn?

Katherine Parr.

Katherine Howard.

Mary Boleyn.

How old was Henry's fifth wife when they married?

Seventeen.

Nineteen.

Twenty one.

When this marriage ended in 1542 which of these
actions did Henry take against his adulterous wife?

Divorce.

Exile.

Execution.

How many times had Henry VIII's sixth wife
Katherine Parr been married before she was selected

as his bride?

Never, she had been determined not to marry unless in love.

Twice, widowed each time.

Four times, three times widowed and one annulment.

When Katherine married him in July 1543 who did Henry know that she was in love with? (Their relationship was halted until after Henry's death when they married.)

Thomas Seymour.

Thomas Culpepper

Robert Dudley, Earl of Leicester.

When Henry decided that his young son Edward would marry Mary, Queen of Scots and thereby unite England and Scotland, the Scots resisted as they favoured a match with France. What was the name later given to the several years of military campaigning intended to persuade the Scots to agree with his plan?

The Rough Courtship.

The Rough Wooing.

The Rough Diamond.

Which of these battles did *not* take place during the above military campaign?

Battle of Pinkie.

Battle of Flodden.

Battle of Solway Moss.

Moments before she died, which of Henry's queen's is quoted as saying:

"And if any person will meddle of my cause, I require them to judge the best. And thus I take my leave of the world and of you all, and I heartily desire you all to pray for me. O Lord have mercy on me, to God I commend my soul.'

Catherine of Aragon.

Anne Boleyn.

Katherine Howard.

Lady Jane Grey, the nine days queen of 10th -19th July 1553, was what relation to Henry VIII?

Second cousin.

Great niece.

Illegitimate daughter.

How old was Henry VIII when he died on 28th

January 1547 at Whitehall Palace, on what would have been his father's 90th birthday?

Forty five.

Fifty five.

Sixty five.

Which wife is Henry buried beside?

Catherine of Aragon.

Jane Seymour.

Anne of Cleves.

Where do they rest?

The Henry VII Chapel, Westminster Abbey.

The Chapel Royal, Hampton Court Palace.

St. George's Chapel, Windsor Castle.

Approximately one hundred and two years later
which king was buried in the same vault as Henry?

Charles I.

Charles II.

James II.

Which of Henry VIII's children succeeded him in 1547 and ruled until 1553?

Edward.

Mary.

Elizabeth.

Which of Henry's wives is shown below?

Catherine of Aragon.

Katherine Parr.

Katherine Howard.

Which wife outlived Henry by the longest time?

Katherine Parr.

Anne of Cleves.

None of them survived him.

Beneath which London palace was the space known as Henry VIII's wine cellar? The cellar survives and today it lies below the Ministry of Defence building.

Whitehall Palace.

Greenwich Palace.

Richmond Palace.

When Henry VIII passed away the news was not

released to the country for a few days so that a regency council of sixteen aristocrats could be installed for new monarch Edward VI.

True.

False.

When was Edward VI's coronation? (The ceremony was shortened as he was a nine year old child.)

20th February 1547.

20th July 1547.

20th November 1547.

With the regency council's agreement Edward VI's uncle Edward Seymour managed his nephew and the country's welfare. He took which title?

Lord Regent of the Realm.

Chief Regent of the Realm.

Lord Protector of the Realm.

By 1549 Edward Seymour was unpopular and to protect his rule – and he said the king's person – he took Edward VI to which castle? This led the boy king to comment "me thinks I am in prison."

Windsor Castle.

Warwick Castle.

Whitehaven Castle.

Edward Seymour was replaced by John Dudley, Earl
of Warwick, the future Duke of Northumberland.
What fate befell Seymour?

He was murdered in his bed in summer 1550.

He was kept under house arrest for the rest of his life
at Somerset House in London.

He was executed for felony in 1552 by Edward VI and
the council.

In 1553 John Dudley, by then 1st Duke of Northumberland, schemed and became the father in law to which lady of royal blood?

Lady Margaret Clifford.

Lady Frances Brandon.

Lady Jane Grey.

Is this a portrait of Edward Seymour, Duke of Somerset or John Dudley, Duke of Northumberland?

Which disease did Edward succumbed to on 6th July 1553 at Greenwich Palace?

Tuberculosis.

Diphtheria.

Dropsy.

What was the name of the document in which
Edward named Lady Jane Grey as his successor?

"The Devise of Pure Rule."

"The Devise of Sanctity."

"The Devise for the Succession."

Which of these people was *not* a godparent of Mary
Tudor, Mary I?

Agnes Howard, 2nd Duchess of Norfolk.

Cardinal Thomas Wolsey.

Thomas Cromwell.

Her relation Margaret Pole, Countess of Salisbury
was appointed as Mary's governess. Which royal
house did Margaret descend from?

Tudor.

Plantagenet. She was the daughter of Edward IV and
Richard III's brother George, Duke of Clarence and
Isabelle Neville.

Wessex.

Mary was unofficially called by which title? She received its associated privileges until Henry VIII decided that she was illegitimate.

Princess of Wales.

Princess Royal.

Princess Regent.

When Henry VIII and Catherine of Aragon's marriage was annulled in 1533 Catherine was forbidden to see Mary. She died in 1536 without seeing her daughter again.

True.

False.

Mary was living at Hatfield House in Hertfordshire with her half sister Elizabeth when Catherine of Aragon died aged fifty. How old was Mary?

19.

24.

29.

Mary's coronation was held on 1st October 1553. It was conducted by the Bishop of Winchester, Stephen Gardiner. Where was it held?

Winchester Cathedral.

St. Paul's Cathedral.

Westminster Abbey.

What other role did Gardiner fulfil at Mary's court until his death in November 1555?

Lord Privy Seal.

Lord Chancellor.

Archbishop of Canterbury.

How old was Mary when she married for the first and only time on 25th July 1554 at Winchester Cathedral?

36.

38.

40.

Who was Mary's husband? She insisted that he reign
as king not as a consort in England.

Philip II of Spain.

Maximilian I of Burgundy.

James V of Scotland.

She suffered from phantom pregnancies but historians have surmised that she had which disease that caused the swelling of her abdomen?

Womb Cancer.

Chrons Disease.

Hyperthyroidism.

Cardinal Reginald Pole was Margaret, Countess of Salisbury's son. He held which role when Mary was queen?

Lord Chancellor.

Archbishop of Canterbury.

Lord Keeper of the Great Seal.

Philip of Spain persuaded Mary to commit English soldiers to a military campaign in France. Which important port did the English lose possession of as result?

Calais.

Le Havre.

Cherbourg.

Mary had which former protestant Archbishop of Canterbury burned at the stake in Oxford on 21st March 1556 with two other prominent clergymen named Latimer and Ridley?

William Warham.

Thomas Cranmer.

Henry Deane.

How are these men collectively known to history?

The Oxford Martyrs.

Mary's Villains of Oxford.

The Oxford Saints.

Mary I died on 17th November 1558. Which of her close advisors died on the same day?

Edmund Bonner, Bishop of London.

Reginald Pole, Archbishop of Canterbury.

William Paulet, Marquess of Worcester, Lord High Treasurer.

Is Bonner, Pole or Paulet shown in the portrait below?

She ordered hundreds of executions of protestants during her reign. Mary was given which nickname?

Bloody Mary.

Burning Mary.

Bag o' bones Mary.

Which wife of Henry VIII was Elizabeth I's mother?

Anne Boleyn.

Anne of Cleves.

Katherine Parr.

On which date was Elizabeth born?

28th June 1533.

7th September 1533.

24th December 1533.

Who was Elizabeth's paternal grandmother?

Elizabeth of York.

Elizabeth of Lancaster.

Elizabeth of Norfolk.

Which palace was Elizabeth born at?

Greenwich Palace.

St. James' Palace.

Richmond Palace.

How old was Elizabeth when her mother was executed?

Just over two and a half years old.

A little over three and a half years old.

Just over five years old.

What did the Second Succession Act do in 1536?

Stated that Elizabeth and her elder half sister Mary were illegitimate and so were not in the line of succession.

Stated that Elizabeth was Henry's heir and that Mary was illegitimate.

Stated that Mary, Elizabeth and any future female issue of Henry VIII were excluded from the succession.

Which of Henry VIII's wives helped to restore

amicable relations between the king and his daughters?

Jane Seymour.

Anne of Cleves.

Katherine Parr.

Elizabeth circa 1546.

Elizabeth grew up enjoying dancing, hunting and which of these other occupations?

Music.

Cookery.

Swimming.

What was the name of Elizabeth's third governess, given the role in 1537?

Catherine Champernowne.

Mary-Kate Herbert.

Elizabeth Leonides.

What surname is she better known by-after her 1545 marriage?

Asherton.

Ashley.

Ackersley.

Who were two of Elizabeth's tutors?

William Grindal and Roger Ascham.

William Grindal and Sir Thomas More.

Roger Ascham and Sir Thomas Howard.

At the age of twelve Elizabeth translated English book
Prayers and Meditations by Katherine Parr in to
which three languages?

French, Latin and Greek.

French, Italian and Latin.

Latin, Italian and Welsh.

Just after Henry VIII's death in 1547 what had an
ambitious Thomas Seymour proposed to Elizabeth?

Marriage.

Guardianship.

A coup to make her the queen.

Thomas Seymour had a habit of visiting the fourteen year old Elizabeth in her bedchamber whilst wearing his nightclothes. What was his aim?

To beat her at late night card games.

To tickle, slap her on the bottom as "horseplay" and to attempt more.

To improve her knowledge of the many portraits in her chambers.

Elizabeth moved to Katherine Parr and Katherine's new husband Thomas Seymour's London home in 1547. Elizabeth 's governess was given a new role.

What was it?

Chief gentlewoman.

Chief embroiderer.

Chief dance mistress.

In May 1548 Elizabeth moved to the home of Sir Anthony Denny, Keeper of Westminster Palace, London with Katherine Parr's strong encouragement. This move ensured that she was away from Thomas Seymour's influence. Where was Denny's country residence?

Cheshunt in Hertfordshire.

Abingdon in Oxfordshire.

Truro in Cornwall.

Denny was what relation to Elizabeth's Chief Gentlewoman?

Brother in law.

Father in law.

First cousin.

Denny was also the keeper of which property that would become synonymous with Elizabeth?

Knebworth House.

Hatfield House.

Gorhambury House.

Henry VIII had already bestowed which property in Hertfordshire to Elizabeth?

Waytemore Castle.

Ashridge House.

The Manor of the Groves.

On 3rd August 1553 where was Elizabeth?

Processing through London with the newly installed Queen Mary I.

She was a prisoner in the Tower of London.

In Hertfordshire, barred from any public appearances by Mary.

What was Mary I's primary reason for disliking and distrusting Elizabeth?

She was jealous of Elizabeth's appearance. She resembled Henry VIII more than Mary did.

Elizabeth was more popular with men than Mary who was thirty seven years old and unmarried.

Elizabeth was protestant, Mary wished her to be a

good catholic.

Who was the leader of a 1554 rebellion to depose Mary I and install Elizabeth on the throne?

Thomas Wyatt.

Wat Tyler.

Robert Aske.

Elizabeth stated that she had no part in the 1554 rebellion but what was Mary I's response?

To banish Elizabeth under guard to Anglesey, an island off Wales.

To have Elizabeth incarcerated in the Tower of London on suspicion of treason.

To move her in to her palace so that she could spy better on Elizabeth.

Who was a surprising supporter of Elizabeth's protests of innocence?

Mary's husband, Philip II of Spain.

Catholic Bishop Stephen Gardiner.

Marie of Guise, Regent of Scotland.

Where did Elizabeth spend almost a year under house arrest during Mary I's reign?

Woodstock Lodge in Oxfordshire.

Middleham Castle in Yorkshire.

Tutbury Castle in Staffordshire.

Whilst at Hatfield House in 1558 Elizabeth learned what about Mary I?

That she had died and so Elizabeth was queen.

That Mary was to relocate to Spain to be with her husband Philip II.

That Mary had secretly converted to protestantism.

What date in 1558 did Elizabeth become queen?

2nd April.

25th July.

17th November.

On which date had Mary I finally and resignedly recognised Elizabeth as her heir?

16th November 1558.

6th November 1558.

26th October 1558.

How long approximately would Elizabeth reign for?

44 years.

54 years.

64 years.

What date was her coronation at Westminster Abbey in London?

15th January 1559.

20th February 1559.

25th March 1559.

Which ruler asked for a marriage to the new queen Elizabeth I?

Cosimo de Medici.

Philip II of Spain.

Maximilian of Bavaria.

Which of these was *not* a name used to describe Elizabeth I?

The Virgin Queen.

Gloriana.

The Immaculate.

Who was Elizabeth's friend from childhood, long term admirer and possibly her lover? She ensured that they had adjoining rooms at her palaces.

Sir Robert Cecil.

Sir Robert Dudley.

Sir Robert Howard.

How did this man's wife Amy Robsart die?

She fell or was pushed down the stairs at their Oxfordshire home Cumnor Place. There were suspicions that it was murder.

Amy died in childbirth whilst her husband was in the Netherlands negotiating a trade deal for Elizabeth.

She fell from her horse when it bolted whilst on a ride in Elizabeth's company.

The first English national lottery was organised during Elizabeth I's reign to raise funds for port construction and ship building. The top prize was £3500 in cash, £700 in plate with tapestries and linen to make the total win £5000 in value. When did the draw take place?

11th January 1569.

22nd March 1571.

31st July 1573.

Where in London did the draw occur?

St. Paul's Cathedral.

Westminster Hall.

Whitehall Palace.

In 1562 which life threatening disease did Elizabeth contract?

Typhoid.

Smallpox.

Leprosy.

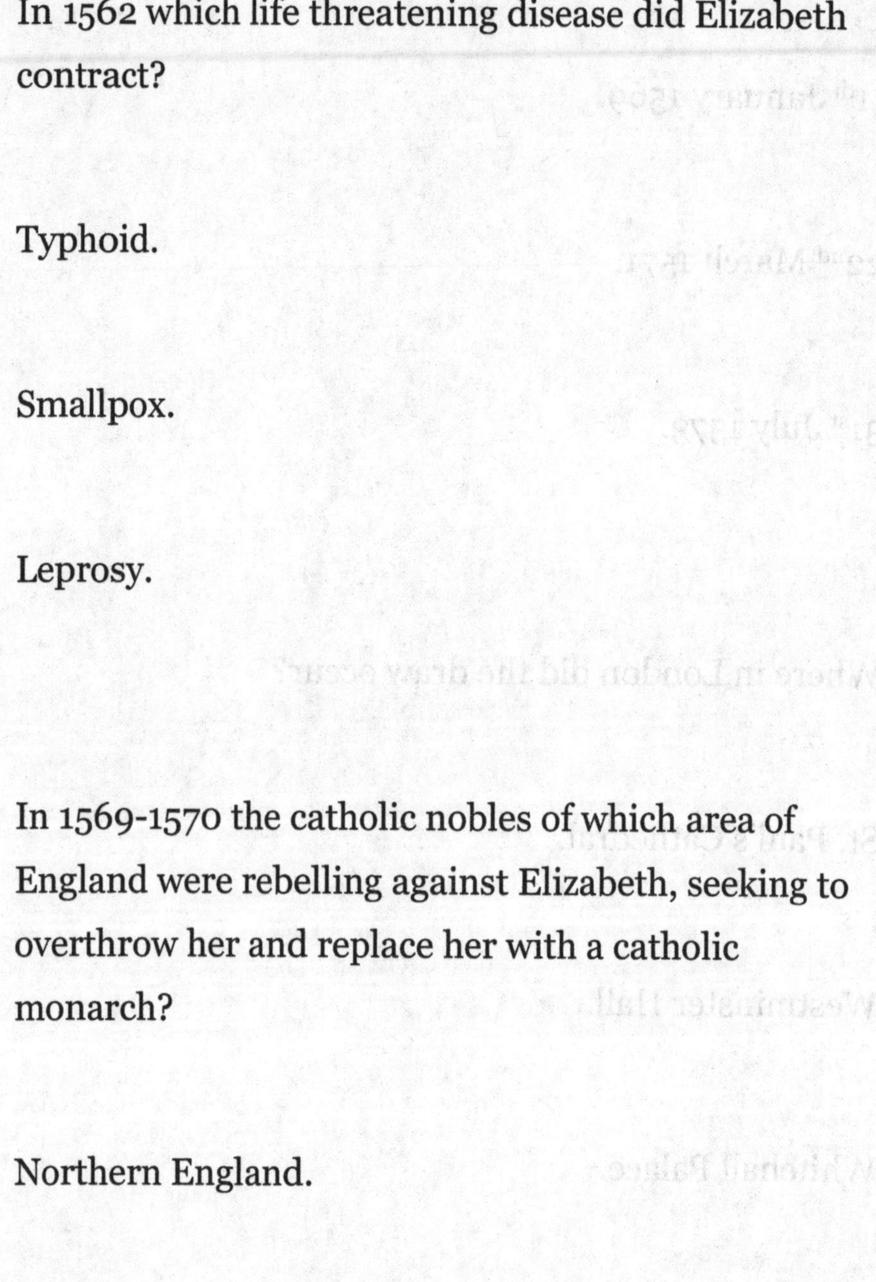

In 1569-1570 the catholic nobles of which area of England were rebelling against Elizabeth, seeking to overthrow her and replace her with a catholic monarch?

Northern England.

Southern England.

East of England.

Pope Pius V excommunicated Elizabeth I in which year? He declared that she was a heretic, the *"pretended queen of England and a servant of crime"* in a papal bull entitled Regnans in Excelsis.

1560.

1570.

1580.

Who was Elizabeth I's close friend who married four times, increasing her influence, wealth and status with each union?

Bess of Rutland.

Bess of Severn.

Bess of Hardwick.

Is this Robert Dudley, Earl of Leicester or his stepson Robert Devereux, Earl of Essex?

Who did Elizabeth offer as a husband to Mary, Queen of Scots so that she had an ally and spy in her Scottish cousin's court? Mary refused to oblige.

Robert Devereux, Earl of Essex.

Sir Francis Walsingham.

Robert Dudley, Earl of Leicester.

What role did "Kat" Ashley hold in the adult Elizabeth's household?

Lady of the Bedchamber.

Comptroller of the Household.

Mistress of the Robes.

Elizabeth married twice.

True.

False.

Elizabeth I's loyal secretary and spymaster was which man?

Sir Francis Walsingham.

Sir Francis Drake.

Sir Francis Tresham.

Is this Walsingham, Drake or Tresham?

Who was Elizabeth I's chief advisor until 1587?

Sir William Cavendish.

Sir William Cecil.

Sir William Carey.

Who took over from him?

Sir Robert Carew.

Sir Robert Cecil.

Sir Robert Constable.

Which cousin and friend of Elizabeth's became her enemy when she married Robert Dudley, Earl of Leicester in the early morning of 21st September 1578 with only a few guests present? (And without inviting Elizabeth.)

Lettice Boleyn.

Lettice Howard.

Lettice Knollys.

Which queen of Scotland was imprisoned in numerous properties around England after fleeing to what she believed would be safety in exile?

Margaret, Queen of Scots.

Mary, Queen of Scots.

Maud, Queen of Scots.

Elizabeth never met this Scottish queen. She feared

that she might like her rival and that would compromise her decision making in the future.

True.

False.

During the Ridolfi Plot of 1571, which catholic Duke planned to depose Elizabeth and rule England as the new husband of the exiled queen of Scotland? No marriage took place. Elizabeth had him executed.

4th Duke of Norfolk.

4th Duke of Rutland.

4th Duke of Wellington.

By the end of Elizabeth's reign how many dukes were there in the English nobility?

None.

Five.

Twenty five.

On which date, after the failed Babington Plot to put the incarcerated Queen of Scots on the English throne, was the ill fated queen executed at Fotheringhay Castle?

8th February 1587.

9th March 1588.

10th April 1589.

How many days prior to the execution had Elizabeth signed the death warrant?

7 days.

3 days.

The same day.

Elizabeth later protested loudly that she had been tricked about actioning the death warrant and vented her anger at her secretary William Davison. She made him the scapegoat for Mary's death and had him imprisoned and fined heavily.

True.

False.

Who is this a portrait of?

Bess of Hardwick.

Elizabeth I.

Lettice Knollys.

Which explorer was the first to circumnavigate the globe between 1577-1580, although this was an unintentional first because he needed to return to England without encountering the Spanish fleets he'd just plundered that were waiting in the Atlantic Ocean?

Sir Walter Raleigh.

Sir Francis Drake.

Henry Hudson.

Which North African country ruled by Mulai Ahmad al-Mansur did England establish beneficial trade and diplomatic relations with?

Morocco.

Algeria.

Tunisia.

In which year did Sir Humphrey Gilbert establish an English colony on Newfoundland to the east of the Canadian mainland?

1563.

1577.

1583.

Gilbert was which English explorer's relative? In 1584, this relative named expansive American territory including Bermuda in honour of Elizabeth I as Virginia.

Sir Walter Raleigh.

John Cabot.

Henry Hudson.

The East India Company was founded under royal charter by Elizabeth I on the 31st December of which year?

1585.

1593.

1600.

"And as nothing is more dear to us than the loving conservation of our subjects' hearts, what an undeserved doubt might we have incurred if the abusers of our liberality, the thrallers of our people, the wringers of the poor, had not been told us!" On which date did Elizabeth deliver her "Golden Speech" at Whitehall Palace, primarily to combat criticism about her awarding monopolies which were then abused. Her speech disarmed many of her critics.

7th September 1588.

31st October 1595.

30th November 1601.

Which playwright became prominent during Elizabeth's reign, often rewriting history to meet with her approval?

William Shakespeare.

John Donne.

Alexander Pope.

How did the maturing Elizabeth ensure that she outshone her female courtiers with her outfits?

She ordered them to wear only black and white.

She banned heeled shoes.

She insisted that they wore fake jewels.

Why did Elizabeth refuse to name her heir? *"...a second person, as I have been..."*

"...is at constant threat of calumny."

"...a focus of plots against her predecessor."

"...is unhappily acquainted with Traitor's Gate at the Tower."

In which year was the Spanish Armada?

1577.

1588.

1599.

The Nine Year's War against English rule in Ireland
was also known by which name?

Tyrone's Rebellion.

The Irish Blarney.

Fermanagh's Fury.

Elizabeth was formally betrothed to Francis, Duke of
Anjou in 1581 after a three years courtship.

True

False.

Which suitor of Elizabeth's is shown in the portrait below? Henry III, King of France, Francis, Duke of Anjou or Archduke Charles II Francis of Austria?

Her regular tours of England were known as what?

Progresses.

Whimsies.

Jaunts.

What was the real name of "Robin" Elizabeth's favourite later in life? She eventually had him executed for treason.

Robert Devereux, Earl of Essex.

Sir Francis Drake.

Sir Robert Cecil.

The Spanish Armada was followed by a 1589 English attack on the Spanish named the Counter Armada. It was a deadly and embarrassing disaster and swiftly erased from popular English historical records.

True.

False.

In 1587 a man named Arthur Dudley was arrested in Spain and was declared an English spy. He claimed he was the son of Elizabeth I and Robert Dudley. He was not believed.

True.

False.

The paste which Elizabeth wore on her face to maintain a pale complexion contained which metal?

Silver.

Lead.

Platinum.

What was the rumour circulated about Elizabeth I
which the Victorians made popular?

She was a witch.

She was a man.

She was not Henry VIII's daughter.

Elizabeth I died on 24th March 1603 at which palace?

Richmond Palace.

Whitehall Palace.

Hampton Court Palace.

In the days prior to her death she had resisted doing what?

Getting in to bed.

Signing her will.

Removing her wig and makeup.

She is buried at Westminster Abbey in a tomb beside which monarch?

Mary I.

Edward VI.

Henry VIII.

Elizabeth I depicted in the 1590's.

The Tremendous Tudors:
Answers.

Henry Tudor, the first Tudor king, was born at Pembroke Castle in Wales on 28th January 1457. What was he known as in Welsh?

Harri Tudur.

What title did the future King Henry VII hold before he battled his way to the throne?

Earl of Richmond.

Who was Henry's father, a half brother of King Henry VI?

Edmund Tudor.

How old was Henry's mother Margaret Beaufort when she became a widow, whilst still pregnant with Henry?

13 years old.

Henry's late paternal grandmother Catherine de Valois was queen consort to which monarch during her first marriage?

King Henry V.

Henry became the senior male heir in which house?

Lancaster.

His uncle Jasper Tudor rushed an adolescent Henry to which area of France for his safety? He remained there for thirteen years.

Brittany.

When Henry travelled to his homeland to claim the throne in 1485, where did his ship moor?

Milford Haven, Wales.

Which battle was fought on the 22nd August 1485? It resulted in King Richard III's death and Henry being proclaimed the new king whilst still on the battlefield.

Battle of Bosworth Field.

Who placed the crown on Henry's head that day?

His stepfather Lord Thomas Stanley.

Who did Henry marry on 18th January 1486 at Westminster Abbey?

Elizabeth of York.

Which emblem was created to mark this union, an end to the decades of dispute about who should rule the country, the Wars of the Roses?

The Tudor Rose.

Name the two best known claimants to the throne who vowed that they were the late King Edward IV's nephew Edward, and Edward IV's second son Richard. Neither succeeded in overthrowing Henry VII.

Lambert Simnel and Perkin Warbeck.

Henry used high taxation, fines and land confiscation from his more wealthy subjects as devices to ensure that no one had the resources to challenge his power.

True.

When Henry VIII became king in 1509 what did he do to his father's chief tax collectors Edmund Dudley and Richard Empson?

He executed them for treason on trumped up charges.

Henry VII lost his wife on the 11th February of which year? This was the day after the death of their nine day old daughter Katherine.

1403.

Where is the chapel built in his name and completed in 1516, that has provided a magnificent resting place for several royals including himself and his wife, his grandchildren Edward VI, Mary I and Elizabeth I?

Westminster Abbey.

Henry was how old when he passed away on 21st April 1509 at Richmond Palace?

52 years old.

When did Henry's mother Margaret Beaufort die?

29th June 1509.

Who did Sir Roland de Velville, Constable of Beaumaris Castle between 1509 and 1535, claim to be?

Henry VII's illegitimate son, born in 1474 to a Frenchwoman.

Is this portrait of Henry VII, his eldest son Arthur or his second son Henry?

His eldest son Arthur, Prince of Wales.

In 1485 Henry created the military corps of ordinary and extraordinary guards stationed at the Tower of London. They are still popularly known as Beefeaters and wear a distinct uniform. What was and is their shortened title?

The Yeoman Warders. In full: The Yeomen Warders of His Majesty's* Royal Palace and Fortress the Tower of London, and Members of the Sovereign's Body Guard of the Yeoman Guard Extraordinary.

*Altered to Her Majesty's for reigning queens.

The future King Henry VIII was born at Greenwich Palace in London on which date?

28th June 1491.

Who was the youngest son of Henry VII and Elizabeth of York?

Edmund (21st February 1499- 9th June 1500.)

Henry VIII's paternal grandmother was which

formidable lady?

Margaret Beaufort.

His maternal grandfather was which king of

England?

Edward IV.

Aged three, which title was Henry awarded?

Duke of York.

Which scholar, philosopher and friend of Sir Thomas More met a nine year old Prince Henry and thought that he had a "certain dignity and singular courtesy" but in later life became wary and disapproving of him?

Desiderious Erasmus.

Henry was a highly intelligent boy, a keen student and an avid reader.

True.

Which of these activities was Henry *not* good at?

Conjuring.

How many years after Prince Arthur's death on 2nd April 1502 was Henry created the Prince of Wales and Earl of Chester by his father?

Within one year, on 18th February 1503.

Which sport did Henry excel at although his father wished that he would not participate because it was dangerous?

Jousting.

How many horses did a contemporary state that the young Henry could tire out during one day's hunting?

Ten.

On which date did Henry VIII succeed to the throne?

21st April 1509.

Which piece of music is Henry VIII credited with

composing even though he didn't?

Greensleeves.

Which of these pieces of music did Henry compose?

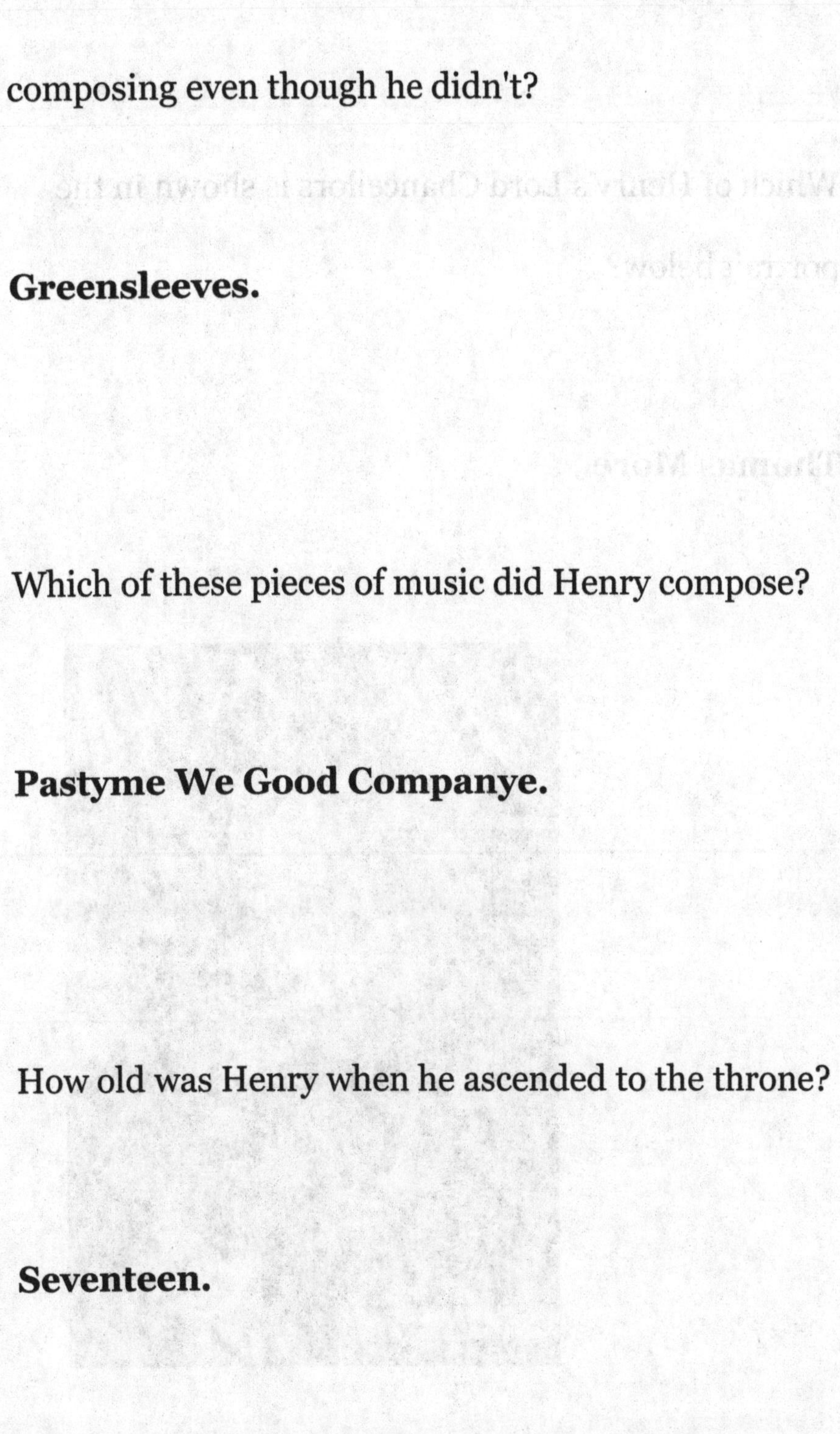

Pastyme We Good Companye.

How old was Henry when he ascended to the throne?

Seventeen.

Which of Henry's Lord Chancellors is shown in the portrait below?

Thomas More.

How many wives did Henry VIII have?

Six.

How many of Henry's wives were beheaded?

Two.

Who did Henry marry on 11th June 1509?

Catherine of Aragon.

What relation was the bride to him?

Sister in law.

On which day did the couple have their coronation at Westminster Abbey?

23rd June 1509.

What name was given to their tragically short lived

son, born on New Year's Day 1511? (And to two other issue who passed away within hours or were stillborn.)

Henry.

What was the name of Henry VIII's eldest legitimate daughter born on 18th February 1516?

Mary.

Courtier Bessie (Elizabeth) Blount was Henry's long term unofficial mistress. She was the mother of his illegitimate son Henry Fitzroy, born on 15th June

1519. What title was bestowed on the boy in 1525?

Duke of Richmond and Somerset.

What happened to this son Henry?

He died as a teenager and was genuinely mourned by Henry VIII.

A celebration-tournament of peace and friendship with frequent foe France was held in Balinghem in Northern France during June 1520. What was the event called?

The Field of the Cloth of Gold.

Shown in this portrait, who was king of France during this event?

François I.

Who gave Henry VIII the title Defender of the Faith?

Pope Leo X.

Which London palace was built on the orders of Henry VIII in the 1530's?

St. James' Palace.

What had sat on the land prior to the palace?

A hospital.

Which college did Henry create at Cambridge University?

Trinity College.

As an adult Henry's height was commented on as unusual. Was he...?

Over 6 feet tall.

Which of Henry's numerous palaces is shown in the image below?

Greenwich Palace.

What other name was this palace known by?

Palace of Placentia.

Why did Henry's first marriage end in acrimony?

After over twenty years of marriage there was no surviving male heir to succeed Henry. He decided that Catherine had to be replaced because their marriage was not blessed and so he would not have a living son with her.

Henry's Lord Chancellor was given the unenviable task of achieving a divorce through the Pope so that the king could remarry. Who was he?

Thomas Wolsey.

What was the name given at court to the question of Henry's divorce and remarriage?

The King's Great Matter.

Charles V, the Holy Roman Emperor at the time of the royal divorce was wholly resistant to it. He was Catherine of Aragon's younger brother.

False. He was her nephew through her sister Juana.

When a divorce could not be secured through the Pope what did Henry VIII do?

He ordered his Lord Chancellor's execution, broke with Rome and was excommunicated. He made himself head of the church of England, divorced and remarried.

What name was given to this period in Tudor history?

The English Reformation.

The Dissolution of the Monasteries, the destruction and sale of church land and property throughout the late 1530's and early 1540's was vital in Henry's eyes to his success. Why?

The Catholic church owned vast amounts of land in England and the monks were loyal to the Pope. They posed a significant threat to Henry's power. Henry wanted the land in the ownership of his loyal courtiers.

Henry's second wife was Anne Boleyn. What was the name of the daughter they had together?

Elizabeth.

What did the Pilgrimage of Grace, an uprising in 1536, call for?

Thomas Cromwell's dismissal as Henry's chief minister. He was the architect of the tumultuous changes in policies and religion.

Why did Henry end his marriage to Anne?

She miscarried a son and Henry was persuaded to believe that she had bewitched him in to marriage and that she would not bear a son.

What other charge was levelled against her?

Incest with her brother George Boleyn, Viscount Rochford.

Anne Boleyn faced trial in May 1536. Who, as Earl Marshal of England was one of the most powerful men present; he delivered the sentence of execution to Anne with no apparent qualms?

Her uncle Thomas Howard, 3rd Duke of Norfolk.

At the tower of London, how was Anne executed?

Her head was severed from her body with a sword not an axe, said to be an act of kindness from Henry VIII.

What date was Anne Boleyn executed on?

19th May 1536.

Thomas Wolsey was replaced as Lord Chancellor by which man who would later be executed by Henry?

Sir Thomas More.

What date did Henry's first wife Catherine of Aragon die on?

7th January 1536.

Which of these forces was Henry VIII credited with expanding substantially during his reign?

The Navy.

What was the name of the famous Tudor ship that first sailed in 1511, was refurbished in 1536 and sank in battle in 1545?

Mary Rose.

What was the sister ship of the above called?

Peter Pomegranate.

Cook Richard Roose was found guilty of poisoning his employer, John Fisher, the Bishop of Rochester in 1531 and also of killing two other diners. The bishop survived. What punishment did Henry decide was appropriate for the cook?

He was publicly boiled alive.

This is a portrait of Elizabeth, daughter of Anne

Boleyn and Henry VIII.

**False. It's Mary, Henry's daughter with
Catherine of Aragon.**

What happened to Henry VIII on 24th January 1536 during a jousting tournament that he was participating in at Greenwich Palace?

Whilst competing, Henry fell and his horse landed on him. After a few hours of unconsciousness the king, who was thought to be dying, awoke. He was left with a painful ulcer on his leg which never recovered and his manner from this point became more aggressive.

Who was Henry VIII's third wife?

Jane Seymour.

This queen bore him a son on 12th October 1537 but died from complications within days. What was the son's name?

Edward.

Who was appointed Archbishop of Canterbury in 1533 and held the role for twenty two years until tried for heresy and burned at the stake?

Thomas Cranmer.

Is this portrait of...?

Cromwell.

Henry VIII placed his infant son in the care of Mary and Elizabeth's Lady Governess. What was her name?

Lady Margaret Bryan.

What did Henry's 1535 and 1542 Laws in Wales Acts
do?

**Officially united Wales and England in to a
single territory.**

How did Henry VIII acquire the nickname
Coppernose?

**Some of the coins that Henry commissioned
and placed in circulation had a flaw. When
the silver gilt on the king's nose was rubbed it
wore off to show that copper, a less expensive
metal, lay beneath the silver top layer.**

What nickname was given to Henry's fourth wife
Anne of Cleves?

The Flanders Mare.

Who painted the portrait of Anne of Cleves that
Thomas Cromwell presented to Henry VIII when
persuading him to marry once again?

Hans Holbein.

In Summer 1540 how did Henry VIII thank Cromwell for arranging the marriage?

He was executed and his head displayed on a spike at London Bridge.

After an unsuccessful few months of marriage Henry demanded an annulment, which Anne of Cleves wisely agreed to. They remained friendly for the remainder of their lives and Henry called Anne which of the following?

The King's Beloved Sister.

With the annulment, Anne was awarded properties including which castle, once home to Henry's second wife's family?

Hever Castle.

Who was Henry's fifth wife? She was a niece of the 3rd Duke of Norfolk and a cousin of Anne Boleyn.

Katherine Howard.

How old was Henry's fifth wife when they married?

Seventeen.

When this marriage ended in 1542 which of these actions did Henry take against his adulterous wife?

Execution.

How many times had Henry VIII's sixth wife Katherine Parr been married before she was selected as his bride?

Twice, widowed each time.

When Katherine married him in July 1543 who did Henry know that she was in love with? (Their relationship was halted until after Henry's death when they married.)

Thomas Seymour.

When Henry decided that his young son Edward would marry Mary, Queen of Scots and thereby unite England and Scotland, the Scots resisted as they favoured a match with France. What was the name later given to the several years of military campaigning intended to persuade the Scots to agree

with his plan?

The Rough Wooing.

Which of these battles did *not* take place during the

above military campaign?

Battle of Flodden.

Moments before she died, which of Henry's queen's is

quoted as saying:

"And if any person will meddle of my cause, I

require them to judge the best. And thus I take my leave of the world and of you all, and I heartily desire you all to pray for me. O Lord have mercy on me, to God I commend my soul.'

Anne Boleyn.

Lady Jane Grey, the nine days queen of 10th -19th July 1553, was what relation to Henry VIII?

Great niece.

How old was Henry VIII when he died on 28th

January 1548 at Whitehall Palace?

Fifty five.

Which wife is Henry buried beside?

Jane Seymour.

Where do they rest?

St. George's Chapel, Windsor Castle.

Approximately one hundred and two years later

which king was buried in the same vault as Henry?

Charles I.

Which of Henry VIII's children succeeded him in

1547 and ruled until 1553?

Edward.

Which of Henry's wives is shown below?

Catherine of Aragon.

Which wife outlived Henry by the longest time?

Anne of Cleves.

Beneath which London palace was the space known as Henry VIII's wine cellar? The cellar survives and today it lies below the Ministry of Defence building.

Whitehall Palace.

When Henry VIII passed away the news was not released to the country for a few days so that a regency council of sixteen aristocrats could be installed for new monarch Edward VI.

True.

When was Edward VI's coronation? (The ceremony was shortened as he was a nine year old child.)

20th February 1547.

With the regency council's agreement Edward VI's uncle Edward Seymour managed his nephew and the country's welfare. He took which title?

Lord Protector of the Realm.

By 1549 Edward Seymour was unpopular and to

protect his rule – and he said the king's person – he took Edward VI to which castle? This led the boy king to comment "me thinks I am in prison."

Windsor Castle.

Edward Seymour was replaced by John Dudley, Earl of Warwick, the future Duke of Northumberland. What fate befell Seymour?

He was executed for felony in 1552 by Edward VI and the council.

In 1553 John Dudley, by then 1st Duke of Northumberland, schemed and became the father in law to which lady of royal blood?

Lady Jane Grey.

Is this a portrait of Edward Seymour, Duke of Somerset or John Dudley, Duke of Northumberland?

Edward Seymour, Duke of Somerset.

Which disease did Edward succumbed to on 6th July 1553 at Greenwich Palace?

Tuberculosis.

What was the name of the document in which Edward named Lady Jane Grey as his successor?

"The Devise for the Succession."

Which of these people was *not* a godparent of Mary Tudor, Mary I?

Thomas Cromwell.

Her relation Margaret Pole, Countess of Salisbury was appointed as Mary's governess. Which royal house did Margaret descend from?

Plantagenet. She was the daughter of Edward IV and Richard III's brother George, Duke of Clarence and Isabel Neville.

Mary was unofficially called by which title? She received its associated privileges until Henry VIII decided that she was illegitimate.

Princess of Wales.

When Henry VIII and Catherine of Aragon's marriage was annulled in 1533 Catherine was forbidden to see

Mary. She died in 1536 without seeing her daughter again.

True.

Mary was living at Hatfield House in Hertfordshire with her half sister Elizabeth when Catherine of Aragon died aged fifty. How old was Mary?

19.

Mary's coronation was held on 1st October 1553. It was conducted by the Bishop of Winchester, Stephen Gardiner. Where was it held?

Westminster Abbey.

What other role did Gardiner fulfil at Mary's court until his death in November 1555?

Lord Chancellor.

How old was Mary when she married for the first and only time on 25th July 1554 at Winchester Cathedral?

38.

Who was Mary's husband? She insisted that he reign as king not as a consort in England.

Philip II of Spain.

She suffered from phantom pregnancies but historians have surmised that she had which disease that caused the swelling of her abdomen?

Womb Cancer.

Cardinal Reginald Pole was Margaret, Countess of Salisbury's son. He held which role when Mary was queen?

Archbishop of Canterbury.

Philip of Spain persuaded Mary to commit English soldiers to a military campaign in France. Which important port did the English lose possession of as result?

Calais.

Mary had which former protestant Archbishop of Canterbury burned at the stake in Oxford on 21st March 1556 with two other prominent clergymen named Latimer and Ridley?

Thomas Cranmer.

How are these men collectively known to history?

The Oxford Martyrs.

Mary I died on 17th November 1558. Which of her

close advisors died on the same day?

Reginald Pole, Archbishop of Canterbury.

Is Bonner, Pole or Paulet shown in the portrait
below?

Pole.

She ordered hundreds of executions of protestants during her reign. Mary was given which nickname?

Bloody Mary.

Which wife of Henry VIII was Elizabeth I's mother?

Anne Boleyn.

On which date was Elizabeth born?

7th September 1533.

Who was Elizabeth's paternal grandmother?

Elizabeth of York.

Which palace was Elizabeth born at?

Greenwich Palace.

How old was Elizabeth when her mother was executed?

Just over two and a half years old.

What did the Second Succession Act do in 1536?

Stated that Elizabeth and her elder half sister Mary were illegitimate and so were not in the line of succession.

Which of Henry VIII's wives helped to restore amicable relations between the king and his daughters?

Katherine Parr.

Elizabeth circa 1546.

Elizabeth grew up enjoying dancing, hunting and which of these other occupations?

Music.

What was the name of Elizabeth's third governess, given the role in 1537?

Catherine Champernowne.

What surname is she better known by-after her 1545 marriage?

Ashley.

Who were two of Elizabeth's tutors?

William Grindal and Roger Ascham.

At the age of twelve Elizabeth translated English book Prayers and Meditations by Katherine Parr in to which three languages?

French, Italian and Latin.

Just after Henry VIII's death in 1547 what had an ambitious Thomas Seymour proposed to Elizabeth?

Marriage.

Thomas Seymour had a habit of visiting the fourteen year old Elizabeth in her bedchamber whilst wearing his nightclothes. What was his aim?

To tickle, slap her on the bottom as "horseplay" and to attempt more.

Elizabeth moved to Katherine Parr and Katherine's new husband Thomas Seymour's London home in 1547. Elizabeth 's governess was given a new role. What was it?

Chief gentlewoman.

In May 1548 Elizabeth moved to the home of Sir Anthony Denny, Keeper of Westminster Palace, London with Katherine Parr's strong encouragement. This move ensured that she was away from Thomas Seymour's influence. Where was Denny's country residence?

Cheshunt in Hertfordshire.

Denny was what relation to Elizabeth's Chief Gentlewoman?

Brother in law.

Denny was also the keeper of which property that would become synonymous with Elizabeth?

Hatfield House.

Henry VIII had already bestowed which property in Hertfordshire to Elizabeth?

Waytemore Castle.

On 3rd August 1553 where was Elizabeth?

Processing through London with the newly installed Queen Mary I.

What was Mary I's primary reason for disliking and distrusting Elizabeth?

Elizabeth was protestant, Mary wished her to be a good catholic.

Who was the leader of a 1554 rebellion to depose Mary I and install Elizabeth on the throne?

Thomas Wyatt.

Elizabeth stated that she had no part in the 1554 rebellion but what was Mary I's response?

To have Elizabeth incarcerated in the Tower of London on suspicion of treason.

Who was a surprising supporter of Elizabeth's protests of innocence?

Mary's husband, Philip II of Spain.

Where did Elizabeth spend almost a year under house arrest during Mary I's reign?

Woodstock Lodge in Oxfordshire.

Whilst at Hatfield House in 1558 Elizabeth learned what about Mary I?

That she had died and so Elizabeth was queen.

What date in 1558 did Elizabeth become queen?

17th November.

On which date had Mary I finally and resignedly recognised Elizabeth as her heir?

6th November 1558.

How long approximately would Elizabeth reign for?

44 years.

What date was her coronation at Westminster Abbey in London?

15th January 1559.

Which ruler asked for a marriage to the new queen Elizabeth I?

Philip II of Spain.

Which of these was *not* a name used to describe Elizabeth I?

The Immaculate.

Who was Elizabeth's friend from childhood, long term admirer and possibly her lover? She ensured that they had adjoining rooms at her palaces.

Sir Robert Dudley.

How did this man's wife Amy Robsart die?

**She fell or was pushed down the stairs at their

Oxfordshire home Cumnor Place. There were suspicions that it was murder.

The first English national lottery was organised during Elizabeth I's reign to raise funds for port construction and ship building. The top prize was £3500 in cash, £700 in plate with tapestries and linen to make the total win £5000 in value. When did the draw take place?

11th January 1569.

Where in London did the draw occur?

St. Paul's Cathedral.

In 1562 which life threatening disease did Elizabeth contract?

Smallpox.

In 1569-1570 the catholic nobles of which area of England were rebelling against Elizabeth, seeking to overthrow her and replace her with a catholic monarch?

Northern England.

Pope Pius V excommunicated Elizabeth I in which year? He declared that she was a heretic, the *"pretended queen of England and a servant of crime"* in a papal bull entitled Regnans in Excelsis.

Who was Elizabeth I's close friend who married four times, increasing her influence, wealth and status with each union?

Bess of Hardwick.

Is this Robert Dudley, Earl of Leicester or his stepson Robert Devereux, Earl of Essex?

Robert Devereux, Earl of Essex.

Who did Elizabeth offer as a husband to Mary, Queen of Scots so that she had an ally and spy in her Scottish cousin's court? Mary refused to oblige.

Robert Dudley, Earl of Leicester.

What role did "Kat" Ashley hold in the adult Elizabeth's household?

Lady of the Bedchamber.

Elizabeth married twice.

False. She never married.

Elizabeth I's loyal secretary and spymaster was which man?

Sir Francis Walsingham.

Is this Walsingham, Drake or Tresham?

Drake.

Who was Elizabeth I's chief advisor until 1587?

Sir William Cecil.

Who took over from him?

Sir Robert Cecil. Sir William's son.

Which cousin and friend of Elizabeth's became her enemy when she married Robert Dudley, Earl of Leicester in the early morning of 21st September 1578 with only a few guests present? (And without inviting Elizabeth.)

Lettice Knollys.

Which queen of Scotland was imprisoned in numerous properties around England after fleeing to what she believed would be safety in exile?

Mary, Queen of Scots.

Elizabeth never met this Scottish queen. She feared that she might like her rival and that would compromise her decision making in the future.

True.

During the Ridolfi Plot of 1571, which catholic Duke planned to depose Elizabeth and rule England as the new husband of the exiled queen of Scotland? No marriage took place. Elizabeth had him executed.

4th Duke of Norfolk.

By the end of Elizabeth's reign how many dukes were there in the English nobility?

None.

On which date, after the failed Babington Plot to put the incarcerated Queen of Scots on the English throne, was the ill fated queen executed at Fotheringhay Castle?

8th February 1587.

How many days prior to the execution had Elizabeth signed the death warrant?

7 days.

Elizabeth later protested loudly that she had been tricked about actioning the death warrant and vented her anger at her secretary William Davison. She made him the scapegoat for Mary's death and had him imprisoned and fined heavily.

True.

Who is this a portrait of?

Lettice Knollys.

Which explorer was the first to circumnavigate the globe between 1577-1580, although this was an unintentional first because he needed to return to England without encountering the Spanish fleets he'd just plundered that were waiting in the Atlantic

Ocean?

Sir Francis Drake.

Which North African country ruled by Mulai Ahmad al-Mansur did England establish beneficial trade and diplomatic relations with?

Morocco.

In which year did Sir Humphrey Gilbert establish an English colony on Newfoundland to the east of the Canadian mainland?

1583.

Gilbert was which English explorer's relative? In 1584, this relative named expansive American territory including Bermuda in honour of Elizabeth I as Virginia.

Sir Walter Raleigh.

The East India Company was founded under royal charter by Elizabeth I on the 31st December of which year?

1600.

"And as nothing is more dear to us than the loving conservation of our subjects' hearts, what an undeserved doubt might we have incurred if the

abusers of our liberality, the thrallers of our people, the wringers of the poor, had not been told us!" On which date did Elizabeth deliver her "Golden Speech" at Whitehall Palace, primarily to combat criticism about her awarding monopolies which were then abused. Her speech disarmed many of her critics.

30th November 1601.

Which playwright became prominent during Elizabeth's reign, often rewriting history to meet with her approval?

William Shakespeare.

How did the maturing Elizabeth ensure that she outshone her female courtiers with her outfits?

She ordered them to wear only black and white.

Why did Elizabeth refuse to name her heir? *"...a second person, as I have been..."*

"...a focus of plots against her predecessor."

In which year was the Spanish Armada?

1588

The Nine Year's War against English rule in Ireland was also known by which name?

Tyrone's Rebellion.

Elizabeth was formally betrothed to Francis, Duke of Anjou in 1581 after a three years courtship.

False.

Which suitor of Elizabeth's is shown in the portrait below? Henry III, King of France, Francis, Duke of Anjou or Archduke Charles II Francis of Austria?

Francis, Duke of Anjou

Her regular tours of England were known as what?

Progresses.

What was the real name of "Robin" Elizabeth's favourite later in life? She eventually had him executed for treason.

Robert Devereux, Earl of Essex.

The Spanish Armada was followed by a 1589 English attack on the Spanish named the Counter Armada. It was a deadly and embarrassing disaster and swiftly erased from popular English historical records.

True.

In 1587 a man named Arthur Dudley was arrested in Spain and was declared an English spy. He claimed he was the son of Elizabeth I and Robert Dudley. He was not believed.

True.

The paste which Elizabeth wore on her face to maintain a pale complexion contained which metal?

Lead.

What was the rumour circulated about Elizabeth I which the Victorians made popular?

She was a man.

Elizabeth I died on 24th March 1603 at which palace?

Richmond Palace.

In the days prior to her death she had resisted doing what?

Getting in to bed.

She is buried at Westminster Abbey in a tomb beside which monarch?

Mary I.

Elizabeth I depicted in the 1590's.